MW01450626

Enjoy!
Melanie Rose

Text and Art Copyright 2002 by Arlene Rose Love.

All rights reserved.

No part of this publication may be reproduced, stored in a retrieval system, or transmitted in any form or by any means, electronic, mechanical, photocopying, recording, or otherwise, without written permission of the author.

Inquiries to ByArleneLove@gmail.com

Follow on Instagram
@ByArleneRoseLove

Prozac is a registered trademark of Eli Lilly and Company.

Platypus Publishing
Title: Will Work for Prozac
Subtitle: A Children's Book for Adults
ISBN: 978-1-965016-30-5

First Printing 2024
Version 2

PLATYPUS
PUBLISHING

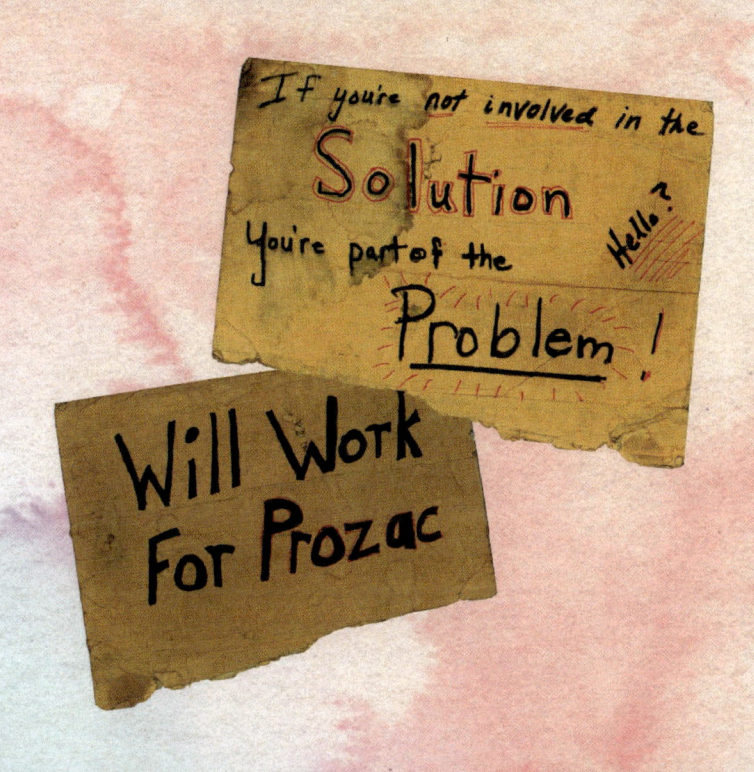

If you're not involved in the **Solution** *Hello?* *You're part of the* **Problem!**

Will Work For Prozac

This all began when I went to the shop of the guy in charge of the Mendocino 4th of July parade to ask for qualification for participation. He asked if I could be there Saturday at 9:30am. I said, Yes! He said, then you are qualified!

During the parade, the people down the street couldn't wait to see what the ruckus was about! Side one brought laughs; side two brought cheers!! What a fantastic day!

Sometime later when I returned to Mendocino, "If you're not involved in the solution, you're part of the problem" had been painted on the side of the firehouse on the main street for all to see.

Dedication

This book is dedicated to Lou C., Seymore, and Bella, all who disappeared off the face of the earth ... coyotes all three. Thank you for wandering with me! You are still in my heart, always!

Also dedicated my children, my grandchildren, and generations beyond. May you be well and live fruitful and healthy lives.

Thank you to my artist, Kate Blalack, for bringing my vision to life. You are one brilliant lady. You were able to illustrate my thoughts in your original water color paintings. Thank you for your meaningful collaboration.

Thank you to Marian Dominquez, the designer, for bringing the whole book together.

And a special thank you to my daughter, Mikel, for being the one who knew how to do this! And my son, Grant, for being there with care and support. I won the jackpot with my children! What can I say?!? I love you both!

Will Work for Prozac

A CHILDREN'S BOOK FOR ADULTS

Written and Conceptualized by Arlene Rose Love
Original Watercolor Paintings by Kate L. Blalack
Book Illustrations and Design by Marian Dominguez

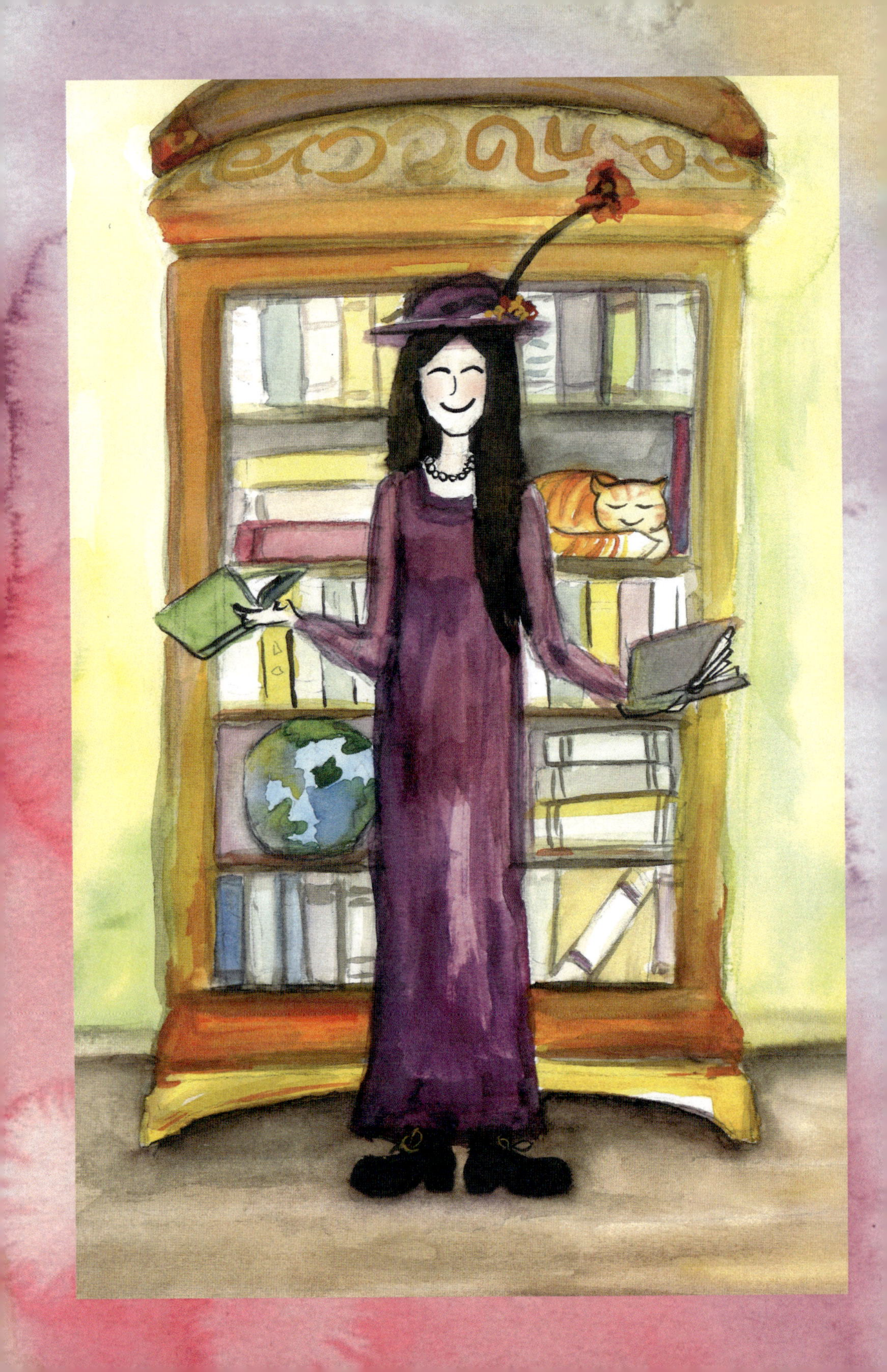

How much longer should I pretend I don't know anything?

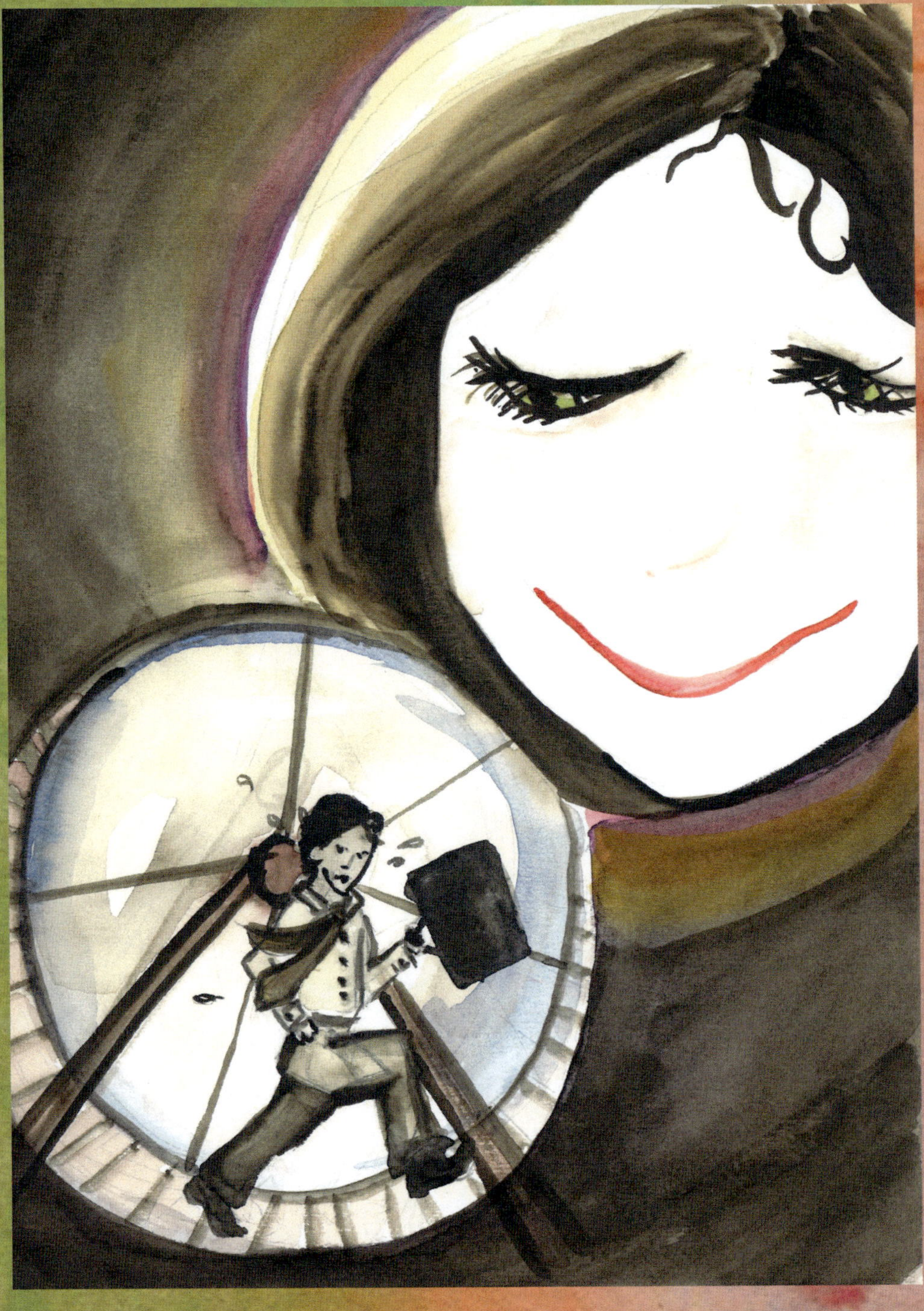

Just because you cannot see what I can see doesn't mean that what I see doesn't exist.

Just because you do not understand me doesn't mean there is anything wrong with me.

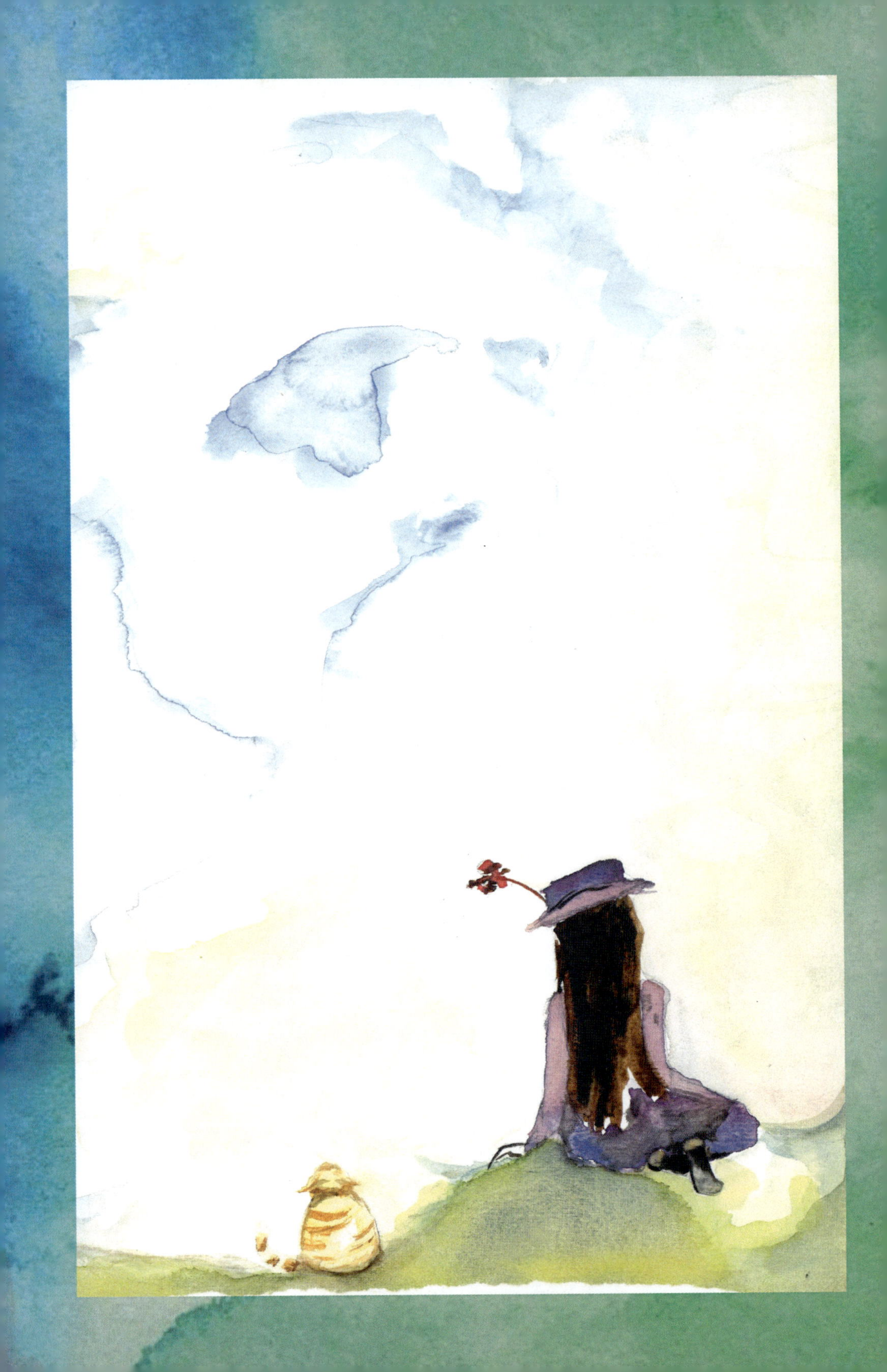

If you weren't so confused you might be able to see how confused you are.

The simple truth is a powerful thing.

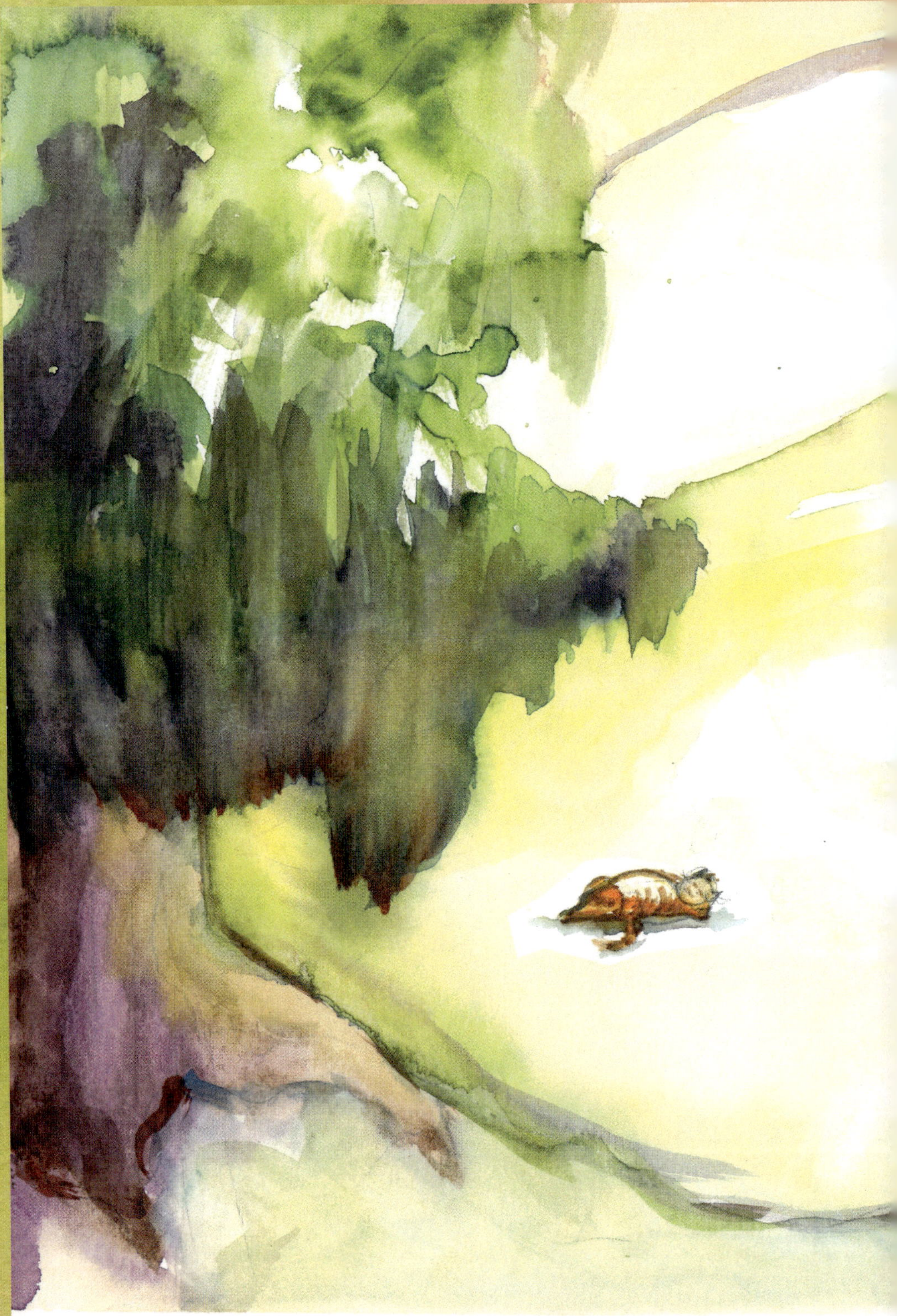

When will the psychobabble end;
I'd like to have my
personality back.

You put me down because I spend
too much time in thought ...
I worry about us
because you don't.

Now that suicide is claiming more lives than homicide, will anyone listen? Who will listen?

Desperation does interesting thing to human beings. Losing your mind is not necessarily one of them.

The leaders are moving forward ... even followers are moving forward, but why are so many standing still?

I've heard that ignorance is bliss ... I wish I could be so blinded.

If you start with purity and innocence, you can best know a man by what he isn't.

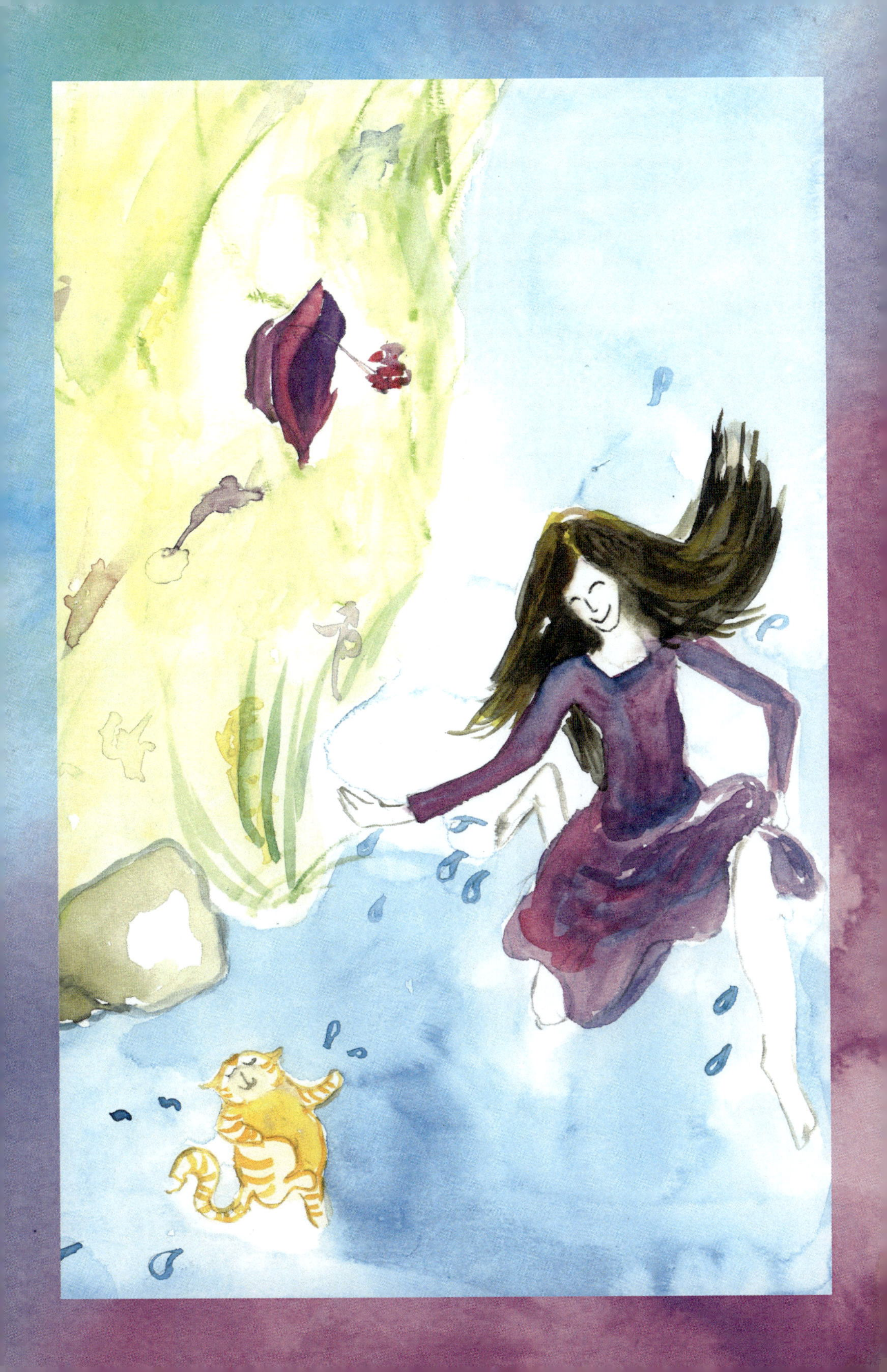

When the channel of giving is open, it's difficult to tell whether you are giving or receiving.

When you're in the practice of serving others it's not difficult to ask for what you need.

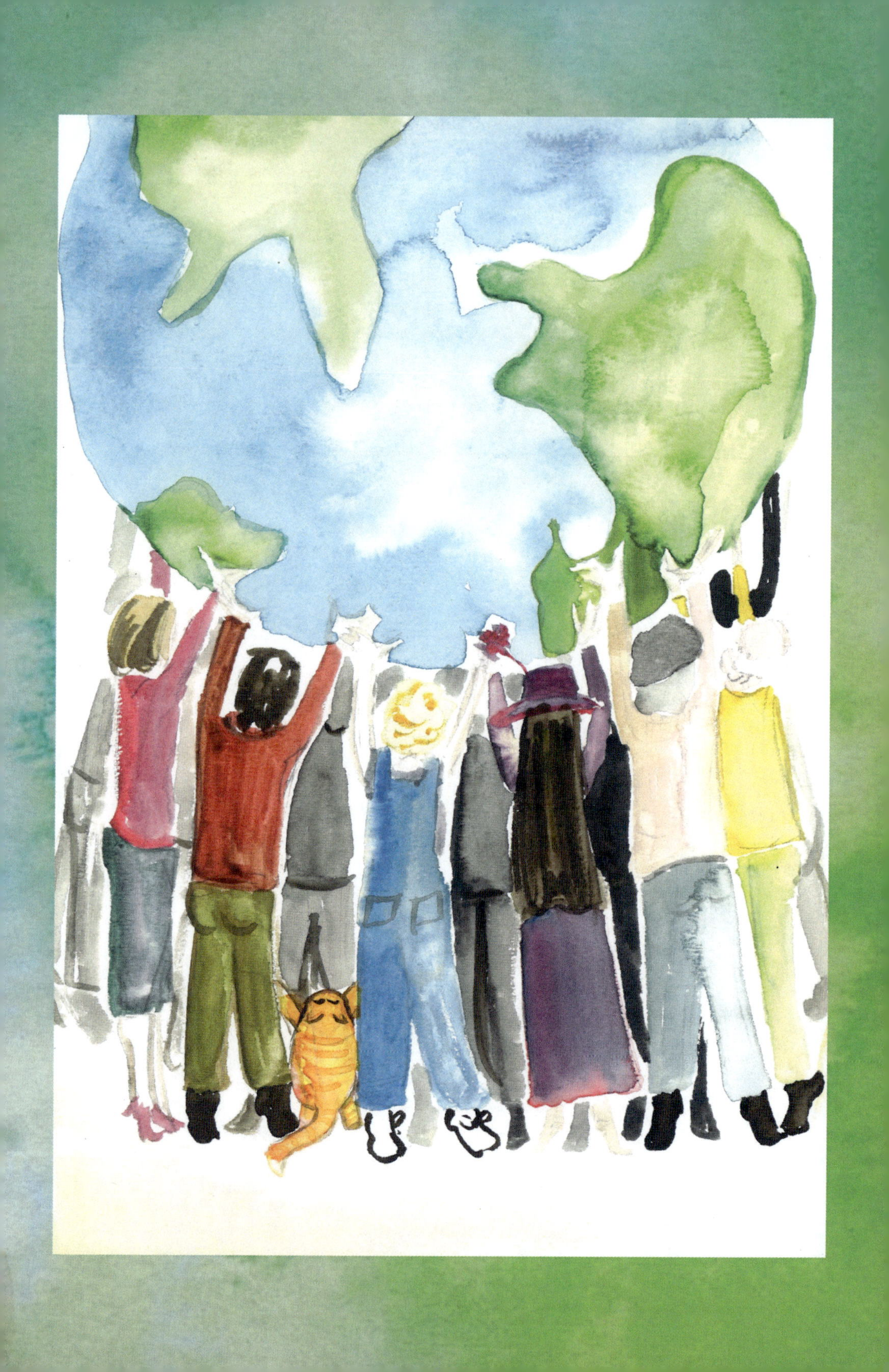

Random acts of kindness? There is a better term for this. It's call teamwork ... and it shouldn't be random.

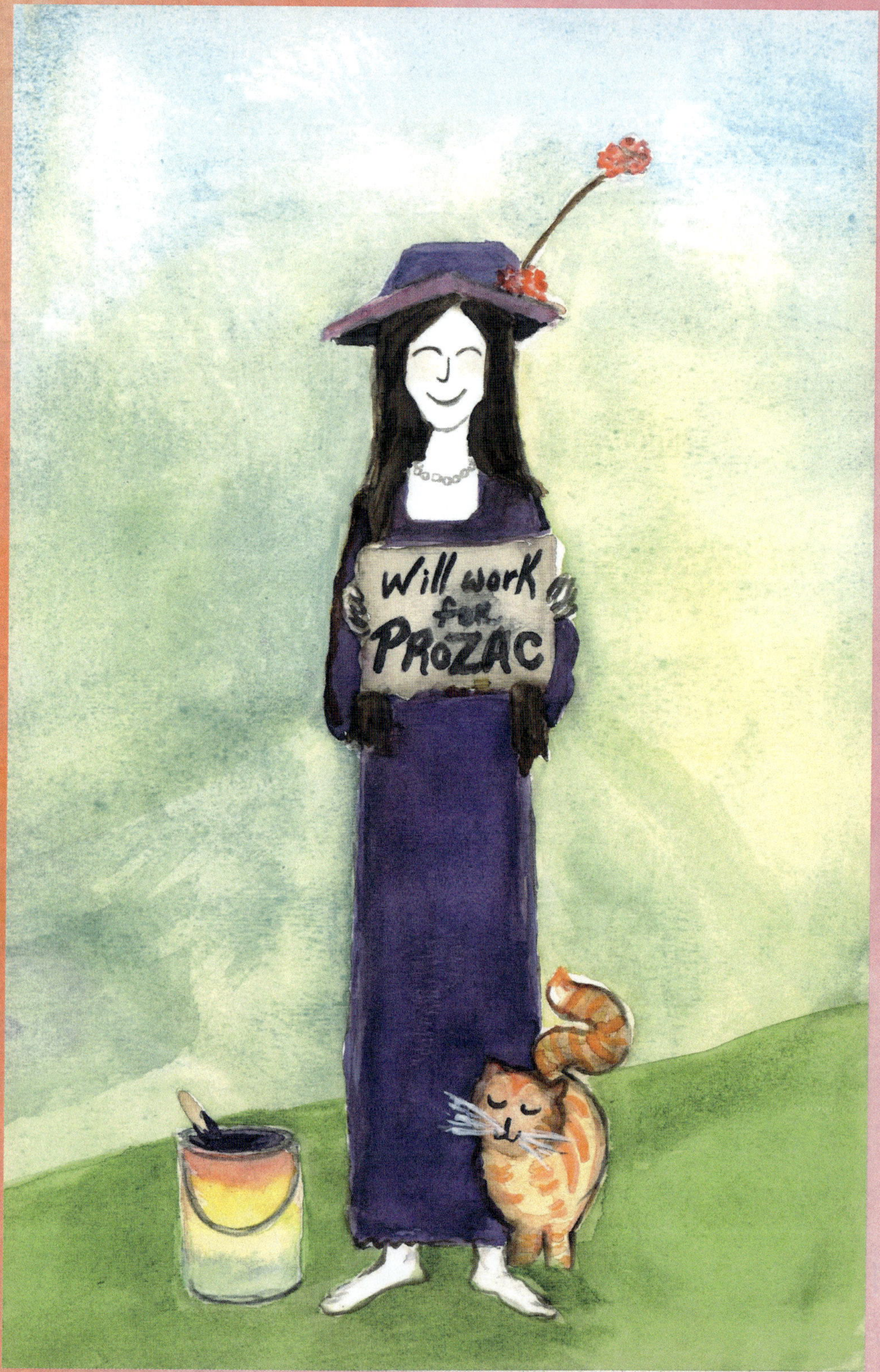
Will work
for
PROZAC

Will Work for Prozac

If you're not involved in *the solution,* you're part of *the problem.*

The author, Arlene Rose Love,
wandering Northern California circa late 1900s

From the Author

From Junior League through divorce and homelessness, I have had firsthand experience of the plight of the oppressed. Will Work For Prozac (WWFP) speaks to those who cannot speak for themselves: the homeless, the meek, the lonely ... the depressed, some on anti-depressants and some who don't have access to the pill for hope. WWFP voices their silent screams of profound common sense in a world where no one seems to be paying attention.

Why a children's book format for adults? In an attempt to reach a vast segment of society who don't/won't read, WWFP is different, better and first. It is my theory that adults who are on or have been on anti-depressants (a significant portion of the adult population) will buy this book in an attempt to communicate with those around them who don't understand that depression is not necessarily a personal issue; it is often a shared condition with the person who suffers and those around them who are unknowingly contributing to the situation. It is time to address the cause of the problem.

I've read at least 1,000 books in the last 25 years covering a broad sense of health and encompassing the entire century. There is nothing new under the sun. WWFP states eternal truths that aren't being applied as often as they should be. In the wake of 9/11 and in today's society, there has seldom been a more important time in human history for these ideas to be conveyed. The world is primed for a paradigm shift.

My formal education and experience since 1971 have focused on Health Promotion/Wellness with an emphasis on Health Behavior. Wellness is the social, physical, spiritual, physical, and intellectual aspects of being human, and is an industry inundated with fads and fraud. But wellness is common sense… even at the graduate level. I have been promoting these commonsense wellness ideas and this book via my homeless wanderings, walking in parades with my sign "Will Work For Prozac," but mostly face to face. In the last 20 years, I have been wandering cities and small towns talking to anyone and everyone and developing a considerable network of friends…people who believe in me and my efforts. I continue to wander and speak of my beliefs pertaining to wellness and hoping for a spiritual awakening of the masses.

This book is the first of many.

Thanks for reading it.

Arlene

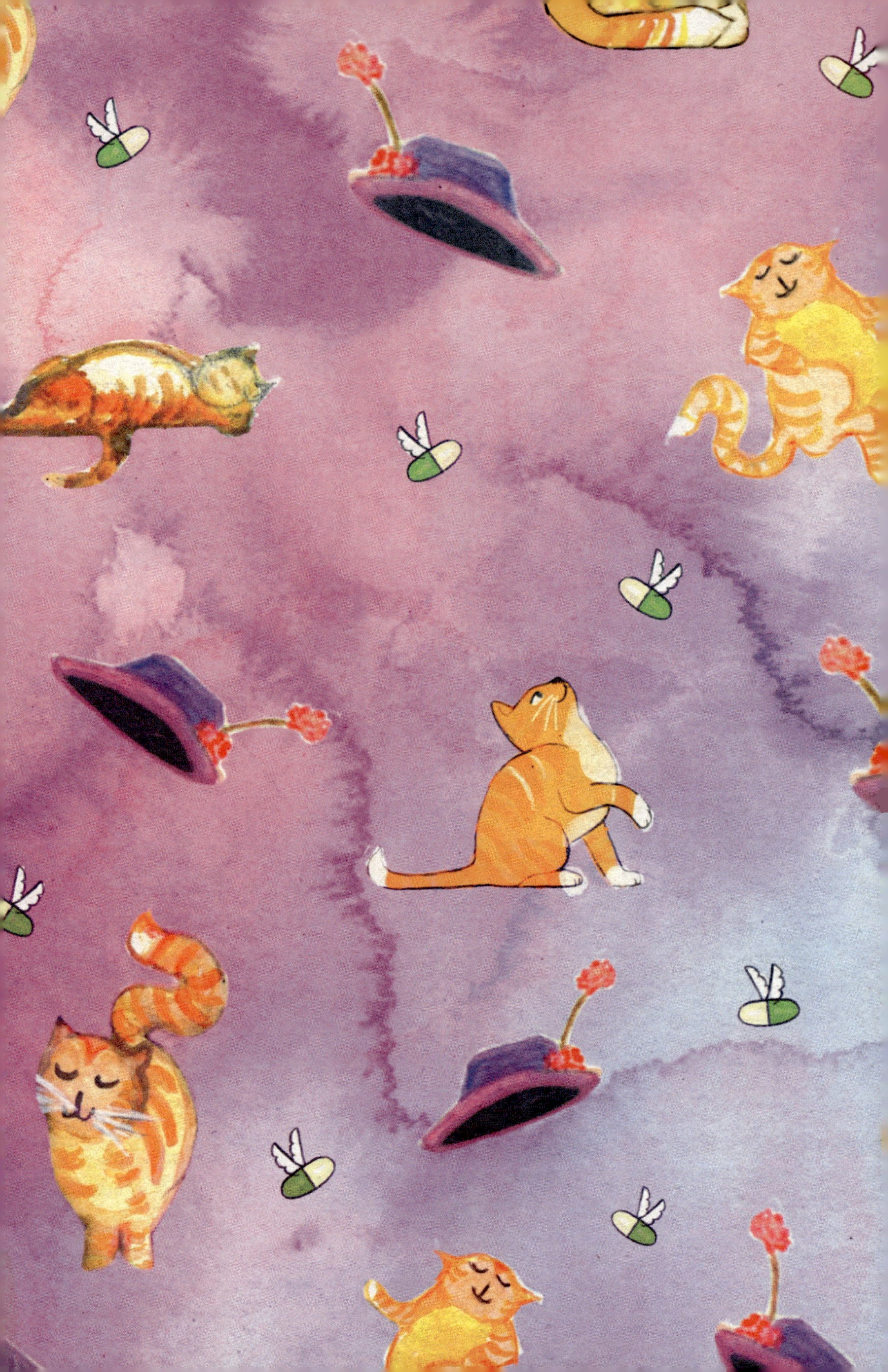

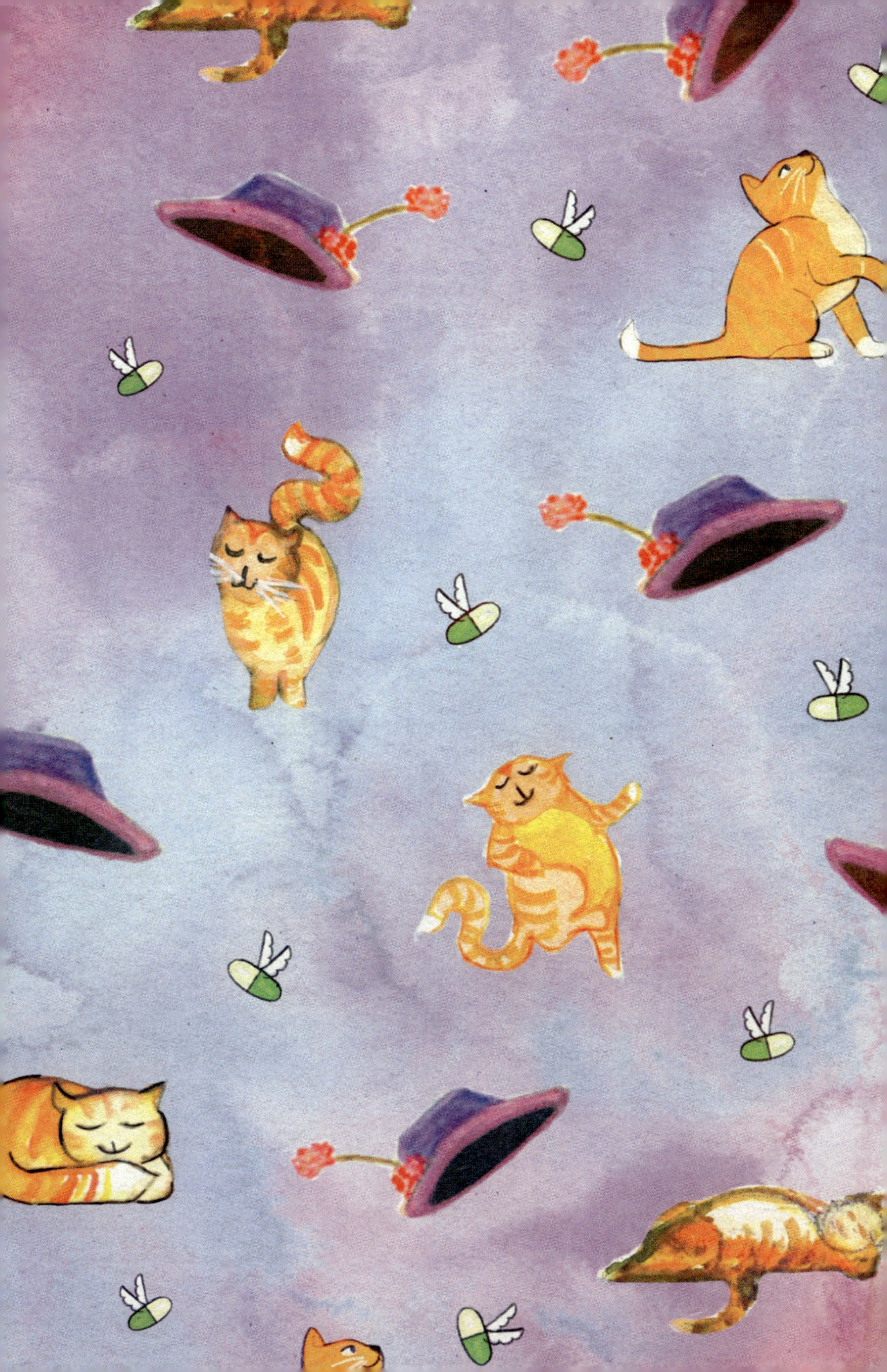

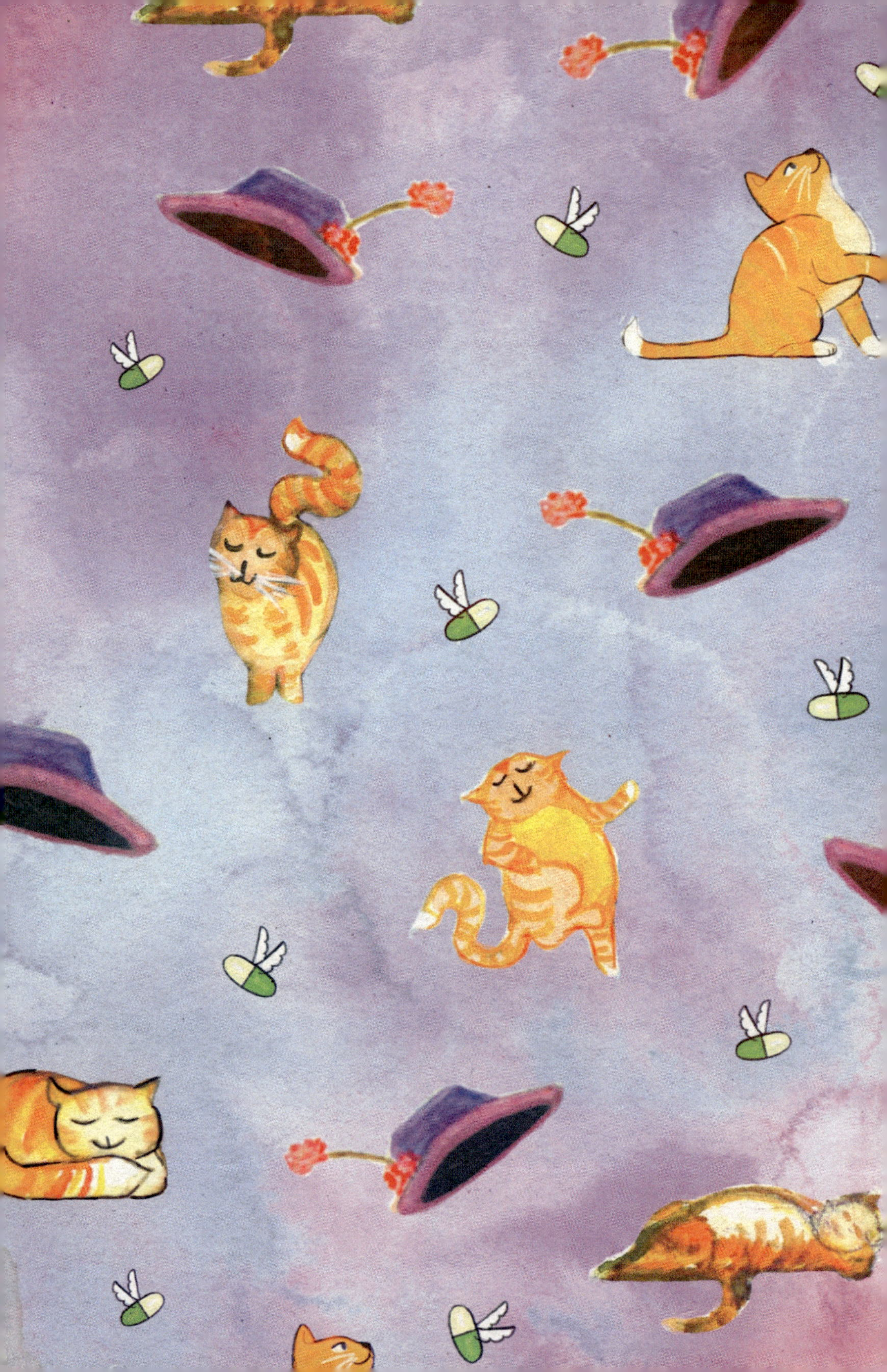